Poetry

2006

by
6th grade students of
Fairfield Middle School

"Where the Best Stuff is in the Middle"

1st WORLD
LIBRARY
Literary Society

Poetry 2006

by 6th grade students of Fairfield Middle School

© 1st World Library - Literary Society, 2005
1100 North 4th St. Fairfield, Iowa 52556
• Tel: 641-209-5000 • Fax: 641-209-3001
• Web: www.1stworldlibrary.com

First Edition

LCCN: 2006936499

SoftCover ISBN: 978-1-59540-886-0

Foreword

Communication is vital in today's society. It comes in many forms these days, from conversing to e-mail. One form of communication is writing, and one form of writing is poetry. Poetry doesn't seem to get the recognition it deserves in this fast-paced world. It is a form of writing that is personal and demands time to read it. It needs to be understood or felt by the reader. It can represent self-exploration for the author, while it can open feelings in the reader. The poem becomes the symbol of communication on many levels to many people. We hope these poems will communicate to the readers in some meaningful way, as they are read.

This collection of poetry was created by the 6th grade students of Fairfield Middle School. It got started when a fifth grade student brought his poem home to his mother to read. His poem had been published in a book like this one. His mother is one of our sixth grade Language Arts/ Reading teachers. She saw it as an exciting project for the sixth graders at FMS. The rest is, as they say... history.

1

This book of poetry communicates to all that take the time to read it. Those who contributed their work hope you will let their poems communicate to you.

The collection of poems in this book started by sharing, and we hope you will share it with others, as you enjoy it yourself.

Gary Henry,
FMS Principal

Introduction

"I write to discover my soul.....I read to discover yours."

The poems you are about to read are written and selected by sixth graders from the Fairfield Middle School in Fairfield, Iowa. These students experimented with many types of poems, including tanka, cinquain, haiku, acrostic, bio, concrete, diamante, ocean research, magazine haiku, couplets, title down, color poems, holiday, and limericks. They did a wonderful job creating poems that expressed who they really are, and I'm proud of their willingness to share this part of themselves with others. I hope you enjoy reading their work as much as I have. They should be very proud of their accomplishments. I am also thrilled for my students to have this opportunity to share their poetry with the world!

Ann Gookin,
6th Grade Language Arts Teacher

Magazine Haiku Poetry

Run!

This man is running
He is Willis McGahee
Now he's with the Bills.

Alex Rodgers

Smellovision

I cannot stand it!
Man, please turn off the TV,
The smell smells awful!

Manda Adam

The looks of the bike
Indian brand is the best
I'd like to ride one.

Zac Simons

Haiku Poetry

Sweet Treat

Gummi bears so good
Chewy, sticky, red and green
Tasty little bears.

Holly Waugh

Oh, Froggy

I lay in the road
I'm hoping not to get squashed
Then a car came by.

Scott Greiner

T-Rex

I like to chase things
I intimidate those things
I am perilous.

Seth Cook

Beautiful Birds

Pruning feather joy
All birds of Iowa do
All birds have beauty.

Skyler Kennedy

Title Down Poetry

Jet Ski

Jetting down the lake
Easy and fun
Time to put more gas in,

Skidding down some more,
Kids watching you
In a terrible fall.

Megan Palmer

Dolphins

Diving down to the bottom
Opening their mouth to eat
Laughing and playing with their mates
Panicking if something happens to them
Hoping to play with mates
Icebergs come down at them
Nothing even happens
Swimming is all they do.

Nikki Schrobilgen

Football

Field goals
On our
Open field
The opponents cried like
Big bald babies
After they
Lost the big game. All because of the
Linebacker blitz.

Doris Jackson

Game

Going to buy some
All the time
My mom says no, but
Every game is mine.

David Rivera

Winter Is Fun

Winter
Is
Nice
Totally
Exciting
Radical

Irritating
Snow

Fantastic
Undislikable
Not not fun snow

Tanner Metcalf

Friends

Friends are fun
Remember
I know
Every time is a
New adventure till the
Day ends and
Save them till the end

Dusty Kingery

Lie

Lazy in bed
Ignored by my friends
Embarrassed to go outside

Cord Schrock

Horse

Happy and jumpy
Oh! Is it fun!
Riding me all day long
So don't forget to feed me
Every day or you won't get a ride

Angela Harrison

Food

Food is very good
Ooh, cherry cheesecake
Oh my gosh, it's so good
Dude, you should try some.

Corey Haynes

Cows

Chaos in the fields
On the countryside
What can I do to save Winnie Fo?
Surely she will win the battle.

Brent Buch

Football

Fighting for the win,
Or fighting for fun,
Ouch, it hurts to get hit,
Time is running down,
But you are speeding up,
All in the stands on their feet,
Lying down, a player is hurt,
Linebacker looks down, and then laughs.

Cody Kool

Laziness

Lounging all day
And night really makes me want to be all
Zippy and happy and do something too bad
It never happens that way
Never will, never have any
Energy to do
Sit ups. All the energy I have is to
Sit and flip the channels on my remote.

Ashley Heninger

Summer

Swimming
Until you get wrinkly.
Much more time outside.
Much more pretty flowers
Everywhere you look
Right, left, and even in trees.

Miranda Williams

Sleeping

Staying in bed all day
Long
Every day and
Every night
Participating in everyday life is not my
Idea of fun
Never doing chores of
Going to school

Andy Phillips

Football

Five linemen
Open a hole for the
Offense to run
Ten yards for the first down
But the defense
Always uses
Linebackers and
Linemen to make the tackle

Alex Gookin

Acrostic Poetry

Christmas

Carols
Hot apple cider
Reindeer
Ice
Sledding
Tamales
Morning shines
Angels
Snow

Mayra Mendoza

Colton Ingle

Courageous
Odd
Late
Tough
Ornery
Nervy

Idiot
Naggy
Generous
Loud
Eerie

Colton Ingle

Limericks

Let's Dance

There was a fat guy from France
Who really, really liked to dance
            He fell down
            And broke his crown
And now he has ants in his pants.

Justin Godwin

At funerals for the dying
Black roses they were all buying
    One seat happened to eject
    The mourner's head was erect
And away he had gone all flying.

Natasha Chang

One day I bought me a car
I drove it a little too far
    My tire it popped
    And my car, it stopped
Then my shoe got stuck in some tar.

Anya Charles

There once were two girls with long hair
One day they went to the fair
    One went on a ride
    Fell off, and then cried
The other didn't even care.

Anya Charles

Once I saw a pool,
It was filled with most awful drool,
But nobody knew
How far it flew
When the pool tripped over a mule.

Julia Larsen

I'm not going to mop the floor,
Or even dust the door.
    Unless you give me money
    And make sweet honey
Because right now I'm poor.

Danielle DeRouen

There was a diner called Fred
And the owner's name was Ned
The diner was so dumb
It made everyone numb
All because Ned was laying in bed.

Trevor Williams

I had a friend named Ted,
His favorite color is red,
    He went on a trip,
    And he took a clip,
When he got back he went to bed.

Felicia Ellis

I had to go to the playground
So we could all mess around.
      When I fell off the swing
      I heard my cell phone ring,
Next time I'll try not to hit the ground.

Davis Lowenberg

There was a man with the last name of Shore
Who had an accident that involved lots of gore,
What happened, you say,
Let's just put it this way,
He will NOT be playing football anymore.

Lindsey Higgins

There once was a kangaroo named May
Who obviously loved to eat hay.
      Sat by a man
      Getting a tan
Eating hay all day.

Haley Williams

There once was a turkey named Gobble,
When he walked he had a funny wobble.
      When he was out walking
      He thought something was stalking
Then he broke his leg and has a hobble.

Taylor Neil

The Girl With The Curl

There once was a girl
Whose hair would curl
    It bounced in the air
    Oh her very curly hair
And around her head it would swirl.

Michelle Spears

Mitten

There was a kitten named Mitten
Who was a sweet kitten
    Until one day
    When it rained
They say, "Mitten lost her mittens."

Dawna Evans

Color Poetry

Black

Black is frostbitten flesh and darkness and dense,
    liquid air.
Black is the taste of sewer waste.
Indifference makes me feel black.
Black is the sound of whispers and evil,
    hardcore music.
Black is a dark basement, a spider's web,
    and the Netherworld.
Everyone dead is black.
Black is pure death and evil.

Aaron McConeghey

Hot Pink

Hot pink is makeup and punk rock clothes
    and feels fuzzy.
Hot pink is the taste of candy.
Cute boys make me feel hot pink.
Hot pink is the sound of loud percussion
    and an electric guitar.
Hot pink is Los Angeles, New York City,
    and San Francisco.
An exciting trip to the mall is hot pink.
Hot pink is being with friends.

Amanda Chatfield

Green

Green is grass and leaves and fields of grass.
Green is the taste of Mountain Dew.
Rides that are too fast make me feel green.
Green in the sound of Green Day and other music.
Green is Green Bay, Wisconsin, and Fun City.
Taking out the trash is green.
Green is Green Day.

Zach Kiefer

Blood Red

Blood red is Kool-aid and food coloring
    and dripping wet.
Blood red is the taste of pop.
Picking on my little brother makes me feel blood red.
Blood red is the sound of blood dripping
    and heart beats.
Blood red is inside a body, in a meadow,
    and in Arizona.
Love is blood red.
Blood red is passion.

Nathan Maynard

Hot Pink

Hot pink is cotton candy and pretty pink nail polish,
and silky smooth.
Hot pink is the taste of watermelon.
Shopping makes me feel hot pink.
Hot pink is the sound of popping bubblegum,
and girls laughing.
Hot pink is the inside of a seashell,
the inside of a candy shop, and the
inside of an ice cream shop.
Being pampered at a spa is hot pink.
Hot pink is frosting, and Double Bubble bubblegum.

Destiny Kennerson

Lime Green

Lime green is kiwis and old 70's style carpet
    and jiggily.
Lime green is the taste of sour apple
    sno-cones. Being dressed up in bright clothes
    makes me feel lime green.
Lime green is the sound of a lawn mower
    and a breeze blowing through the trees.
Lime green is a garden, meadow, and a flower shop.
    Giving facials at a slumber party is lime green.
Lime green is a sour apple Jolly Rancher.

Dana Melcher

Black

Black is pupils in the night sky and Oreos in my
  cookie jar and black sticky tar.

Black is the taste of dark chocolate.

Hatred makes me feel black.

Black is the sound of death, and bats echoing
  in the night.

Black is dark alleys, funeral homes and dark,
  lonesome and bitter-like Hell.

The thought of death is black.

Black is dying roses of love.

Mathew Whitten

Petal Pink

Petal pink is blush and roses and soft and silky.
Petal pink is the taste of pink lemonade.
Being loved makes me feel petal pink.
Petal pink is the sound of laughing and birds chirping.
Petal pink is a garden, a flower shop, and a coral reef.
Being pampered at a spa is petal pink.
Petal pink is being with friends.

Chelsea Haynes

Things Found Poetry

Things Found in an Attic

Spiders crawling everywhere,
Cobwebs getting in your hair.
Old clothing on racks,
Everywhere you see bats.
Dust that makes you sneeze,
People in pictures saying, "Cheese!"
Old furniture falling apart,
Cheap toys from K-Mart.
Rotting floors from termites,
Bad flashbacks from 70's nights.
Stuff you're too embarrassed to show,
Ghosts of relatives you don't know.
Clothing that you thought was cool,
Back in the 80's, old school!

Tori Ogden
Lindsey Higgins
Andrew Kessel
Mukund Martin

Things Found in a Closet

1. posters
2. games
3. stuffed animals
4. shoes
5. boxes
6. broken CDs
7. junk in the trunk
8. Barbie doll heads
9. a couple F papers
10. rug
11. 2-week-old slice of pizza
12. fake hair
13. fart machines & whoopee cushions
14. bean bag chair
15. lava lamp
16. my fat cat
17. dirty underwear
18. soda bottles
19. old magazines
20. clothes

**Summer Terrell, Natasha Chang
Maggie Carlos, Allison Hoffman**

Things Found In A Teenager's Room

A queen-sized bed,
Some gel for your head.
A television with a DVD player,
A surround-sound with lots of power.
Pillows and clothes on the floor,
50 Cent on the door.
Love sack on the ground,
The remote that I found.
In the middle a chair,
On the bed a bear.
On the stand a stereo,
On the ground a Cheerio.

Troy Lyons
Cody Kool
Doris Jackson
Cord Schrock

Things Found At The Skating Rink

1. Candy bars
2. And valentines
3. Numbered walls
4. And stuffed dolls
5. Video games
6. And lots of names
7. People dancing around the floor
8. And lots of sores
9. Look at that couple going fast
10. Slushies
11. Wheels go round
12. Music pumpin'
13. People jumpin'
14. Disco balls
15. And flashing lights
16. Moonlight dancing and people prancing!
17. Each person has these on their feet
18. At this place where people meet!

Kelsie Moore
Destiny Kennerson
Abi Messer
Scoti VanHemert

Jobs For A Teenager To Do

Wal-Mart
Hy-Vee
McDonald's
Family Restaurant
Sonic
Fazolies
Wendy's Family Video
They can't be:
Doctor
Dentist
Scientist
Teacher
Director

Taylor Clemons
Tyler Breeding
Trevor Williams

Things Found In A Teenager's Closet

1. Shoes
2. Clothes
3. Stuffed Animals
4. Dirty Laundry
5. Smelly Socks
6. Dust Bunnies
7. Spilled Make-up
8. Books
9. Oh, my gosh! What is that moving? Never mind, I don't want to know!
10. Pop Bottles
11. Sticky Gum
12. Candy Wrappers
13. Hair Ties
14. Papers
15. Notes
16. Missing Homework
17 Overdue Library Books
OH MY GOSH! ISN'T IT MESSY!

Summer Fritz
Dusty Kingery
Felicia Ellis, Mayra Mendoza

Tanka Poetry

The Wonderful Day

Prairies blowing wild,
Horses running in the wind,
Watching clouds float by,
Family picnics in the sun,
The sun is brightly glowing.

Summer Terrell

A Tanka Poem

Midnight Club 3 Dub,
Making your cars really fast,
Making your car bounce,
Making your cars look tricked-out.
Beat the game, then use cheat codes.

Kyle Tramontana

Mom

My mom is so cool
My mom's name is Dawn Minear
She is very sweet
A loving, caring person
I love my mother so much.

Skyler Bartholomew

My Motorcycle

My motorcycle
Goes very fast and is loud.
It is exciting.
It is rushing to ride it.
It is very fun to ride.

Austin Wilkinson

Praying Mantis

Preying on the prey
Watching from a rosebush
Getting so, so close
Then strike and grab on to it
Then watch and eat it alive.

David Franklin

Cows

Cows have many spots
Wandering through the pastures
Having fun, no doubt
Some cows look like sheep to me
Even though sheep are smaller.

Kaylen Marlay

A Tanka Poem

The snow rains from clouds
Freezing all the trees and grass
Very cold to play
The sun comes out of the clouds
Now summer, here we come. Yea!

Corina Morgado

Couplets

I like to eat Chinese rice,
I think it is very nice.

I wish I was an Orca whale,
Then I cold splash my great tail.

I want to be a Porcupine fish,
I just hope I am not put on a dish.

I really like my brother's steaks,
But there is enough blood to fill a lake.

I used to own an orange cat,
But now he is as flat as our welcome mat.

Jon Fulton

I love games about WW2
Oh, wait, I saw one that's really new.

I love my cute little kitty cat
But he is getting really fat.

I once had a funny cat
My sister said he looked like a rat.

I once drove a car really fast
But that put me in a big body cast.

Shut up, you stupid dog
He barks 24/7, even in the fog.

Tyler Breeding

I promise you my dear friend
When you're down, I'll give you a lend.

You know I tell no lies
And you know I don't say good-byes.

I know you love me as I do you
Our love's forever, our love is true.

When you're holding my hand by my side,
I open myself up, and reach out wide.

When we touch and when we embrace
I get so happy by looking at your face.

All the times we treasure and share,
There isn't a day that you're not there.

Lucinda Wymer

Diamanté Poetry

Light and Dusk

Light
White, day
Loving, caring, snowing
Noon, love, hate, midnight
Scaring, hating frightening
Black, night
Dusk

Shannan Baker

Predator and Prey

Predator
Hunter, fisher
Running, eating, galloping
Killer, catcher, dead, bones
Fighting, hiding, watching
Guarder, swimmer
Prey

Dustin Burke

Cat and Mouse

Cat
Big, proud
Spying, pouncing, cleaning
Lion, tigers, Jerry, Nibbles
Sneeking, hiding, stealing
Small, scared
Mouse

Dallas Guffey

Ocean Poetry

Venomous

I'm the blue-ringed octopus,
    I'm only about four inches tall.
I'm blue and yellow colored,
    I have blue rings that show when I attack,
And poison that kills.
    Two different poisons,
One for prey and predators,
    And one for self-defense.
I live in seashores and offshore reefs,
    I can live 130 feet deep.
I eat crabs, hermit crabs, mollusks, and shrimps,
    I have to watch out, or I'll be eaten by whales.
My poison is in my saliva,
    It contains textrodotoxin.
I live in southern Australia,
    You better watch out for my venomous poison.
I'm the blue-ringed octopus.

Tori Ogden

Rock Hopper Penguin

I am a Rock Hopper penguin,
I eat krill and slide down hills.
I swim 25 miles per hour to catch my prey,
And I come to shore to rest and breed.
The feathers on my head are bright in the light.
If you get close, I'll stay or run away.
You can find me in a pool or in a zoo.

José Heilmann

Monster of the Deep

I am the Orca.
My skin is rubbery.
My skin is black and white.
I swim all around the world.
I crunch upon Weddell Seal.
I can weigh 13,200 pounds, and
I use echolocation to find some prey.
You don't want to mess with me!

Matthew Burnstedt

Concrete Poetry

Balloon

```
            going
         going going
       higher and higher
       and higher, getting
      smaller and smaller
     and smaller until ir's
      o n l y  a  tiny d o t
       in the sky, almost
        gone…now it's
         gone.  Well,
            now
                 it
                  is
                   t
                    i
                     m
                       e
                        to
                         l
                          e
                           t
                        go
                  of
                a
                  n
                   o
                    t
                     h
                      e
                       r
                            balloon….
                              going
                                going
                                   gone!
```

Mukund Martin

103

A Rain Droplet

Gently falling from the sky... Oops...it fell on my head with a plop!

Tommy Price

Holiday Poetry

Christmas Time

Carols are heard mostly on Christmas night.
    Many people like to sing carols.
The delicious smell of that hot, spicy apple cider!
If you are a good listener, you might be able to hear
    Santa's eight reindeer.
Be careful if you go outside, because one step,
    you fall on ice!

Sledding is fun, sledding is great,
Be careful, don't break an arm or your leg!
Sweet, sweet smelling tamales are great for a cold
Christmas!
On Christmas morning it shines! It is just beautiful!
On Christmas it is just great to make snow angels.
The snow is just beautiful and sparkling for
    children to play.

Mayra Mendoza

Colors Of Christmas

I love the colors of Christmas!
>Red—For the suit on Santa
>Green—For the Christmas trees standing tall
>Silver—Is the shiny bow on top of
>all my presents
>White—Is the snow on the ground
>Gold—For the gold wrapping paper.

Michael Gookin

Poems From the Heart

Believe

I can do anything,
If I find it in my heart.
I can do anything,
That's what sets me apart.
I could touch the moon,
If I wanted to.
People who look,
But never find,
People who don't,
Believe in their mind.
I could be on top of the world,
But I'm just an ordinary girl.
God gave us eyes,
But why can't we see?
What really lies beneath,
If you look into your heart,
That's what sets you apart.

Serena Ward

A Cheer for Chairs

All i do is sit around,
I'm a couch potato.
All i do is watch the clock,
waiting for it to strike 5:00.
I have towels on my arms,
and a pillow on my seat.
I have a few socks under my covers,
from some dirty feet.
The dog being a bad boy,
has chewed me up like meat.
I can't stand another day,
although i wish i could.
Seats never stand,
but i think they should.

Serena Ward

It was a great experience,
Probably the best of my life.
I was staring a the court next to his wife,
He would scream and the team would listen.
Never held state on the floor that glistened,
The thing that brought me to my knees,
Was what he said in the locker room.
Something I will not share,
And never will.
Because how much of this paper,
Are a few tears going to fill?

Serena Ward

If Poetry.....

If lonely is just a word,
It cuts like daggers;
If sorrow is only a black hole,
That's in your stomach,
If happiness is always bold,
Then where did it all go?
If feelings are just poetry,
Then I've let you into my heart.
If believing is just a myth,
Then I am a legend.
If paper and pen are a way to get through,
And thinking is a path to your soul.
Then I've been swallowed whole.

Serena Ward

www.ingramcontent.com/pod-product-compliance
Lightning Source LLC
LaVergne TN
LVHW091156080426
835509LV00006B/714